Your 60 Minute Lean Business

Kaizen Mindset

Your 60 Minute Lean Business

Kaizen Mindset

May 2013

First Edition

www.lulu.com

ISBN: 978-1-304-05322-0

Also by Jason Tisbury:

Your 60 Minute Lean Business:
5S Implementation Guide
Total Productive Maintenance
Standardized Work

7 Steps To A Lean Business

Contents

Foreword

Welcome to the Lean Business in 60 Minutes series of books. Why 60 minutes? Well for a couple of reasons. It occurred to me a number of years ago while searching through libraries and book stores for texts on the topic of lean manufacturing and lean business that most of the available books were quite large and often not easy to understand for someone new to the topic. The essence of lean is to remove waste from a business and its processes, yet here were all of these books that were filled with non-essential words – waste. I felt a book on the topic of lean should itself be lean. With this in mind I went about writing my first book on lean – 7 Steps To A Lean Business – an overview of lean manufacturing and lean business systems. At 140 pages, this book can be read in a couple of hours and while the details may not enable one to immediately turn a business lean, I believe 7 Steps does provide a very sound overview and ground learning for the lean newcomer.

Now it is time to share the details of some of the different lean tools, I started writing a book detailing all of the tools but soon realised what I was writing wasn't lean enough. And so the Lean Business in 60 Minutes idea was conceived. Starting with 5S and TPM, the series is now working through the Lean House.

If you are a business owner or manager and are looking for a concise, detailed guide to understanding the kaizen mindset, then this book was written especially for you. My goal is to share what I have been lucky enough to learn with other like minded people who may not have had the dumb luck that I have had. When I say dumb luck, I mean dumb luck. The following is the story of how I came to learn lean, I'm sharing this story to firstly build my credentials and secondly to show how anybody can learn and implement these tools.

At the age of 32 I was working in a factory after a recent business failure when I was lucky enough to break two fingers in a ten ton press. It was quite a bad break, twelve months recovery including two surgeries (one bone graft). Now it may seem strange to call that lucky, but luck is what you make of a situation. Even though I had only one working hand, I could still use a computer, and I was fairly handy on a computer (pun not intended). I ended up working with the Quality Manager who by chance was starting to implement some lean manufacturing / continuous improvement ideas in the business. I learnt a great deal during this time. I was also lucky that this company was in the automotive industry and that one of their main customers was Toyota, probably the best company in the world to learn from. I spent the next five years living and breathing the Toyota Production System (TPS) with direct instruction and mentoring through Toyota. Now after having implemented lean systems and tools through a variety of companies in many organizations in many diverse industries, it is time to share what I have learnt for others to benefit.

What is Kaizen?

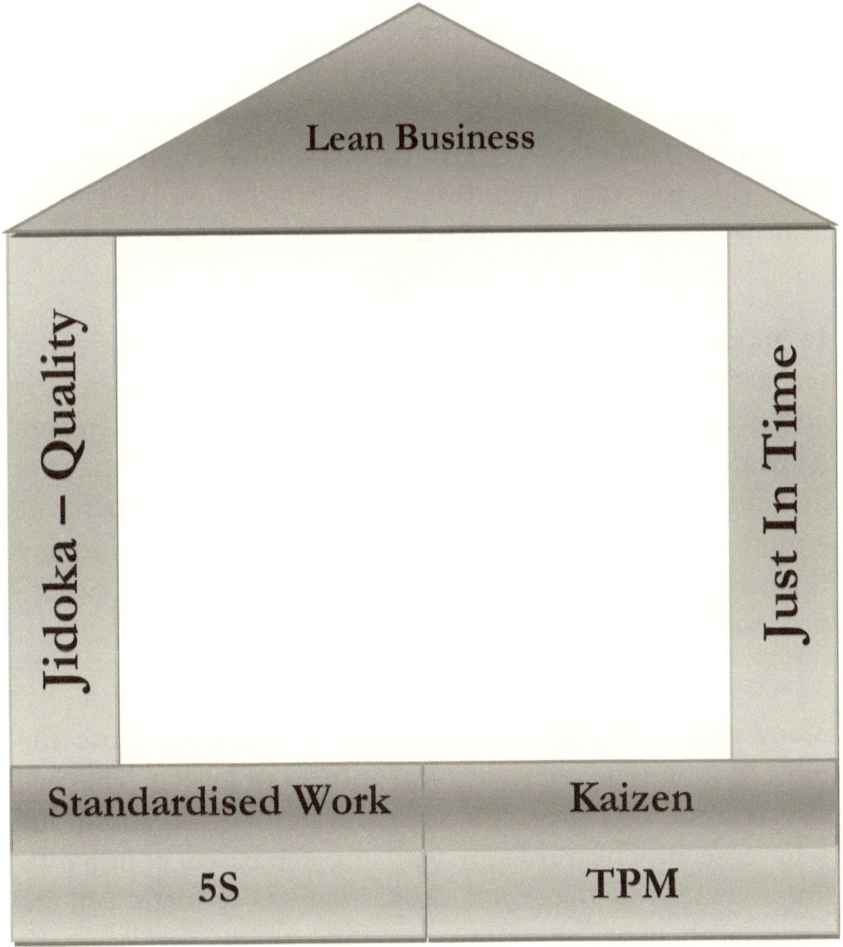

Translated, kaizen simply means improvement, however in practice it is continually improving the work practices.

Where Lean is a business or management system aimed at continuously improving the value delivered to the customer, kaizen is a method for delivering this improvement and becomes very much a mindset and a part of daily life. In the best examples of Lean this practice is seen from the CEO to the cleaner, every employee (and even contractors) are encouraged to experiment with their processes to identify small improvements. Over time, these small improvements add up to very significant improvements delivering improved quality, safety, satisfaction and profits.

In modern business management textbooks this is often taught as "innovation", this is quite different to kaizen as it encourages and focuses on large scale improvements (similar to Six Sigma Projects) delivering significant financial benefits. Kaizen in contrast is incremental improvements at a more micro level that are not always directly linked to any financial benefit and could simply deliver an "easier" process.

Many organizations in English speaking countries use the term "continuous improvement" instead of kaizen. This has also become very project based work in many organizations I have seen. The problem with project based continuous improvement is that once again there is a focus on the financial benefit or return on investment (ROI); don't misinterpret, there is a definite need for financial benefit to an organization. It's just that by focusing on finances alone, we miss out on so many other benefits; and it is often these "other" benefits that turn into the biggest and best opportunities in the future.

Where kaizen differs from these project types of improvement is in the size of the improvements and the drive of the improvements. By making a small improvement today that makes a difficult job a little easier you have engaged the employee; they are likely to be more productive and have greater buy-in to the organization. This will deliver further incremental improvements which will compound into significant improvements to quality, safety, return etc.

Kaizen is a way of life, it is not a project.

What is a kaizen mindset?

Is it a culture? Culture is a funny thing, lately I have been hearing about culture change almost daily. A culture is something that is developed; not made or changed at will in my opinion. Culture is the outcome of beliefs, behaviors and values; of these I would say the behaviors is the most telling. As organizations, we are often very good at developing organizational visions and values, how good are we at measuring our behaviors against those values? Often not very good! The only way to achieve a culture change is through changing the behaviors across the organization – starting with the top! Back to the question; yes a kaizen mindset is a cultural thing so to develop a kaizen mindset in your organization you have to start with the behaviors and conversations at the top. You can tell a lot about an organization by listening to the conversations that take place, especially those at the senior level. Are they strategic or operational? Are they solving problems or looking for whom to blame? Are they asking the right questions and focusing on the right outcomes? The answers to these questions are a good indicator of the culture of the organization; a far better indicator than the values printed and hung on the wall in the foyer!

So what is a kaizen mindset? It is an organizational value and behavior. What does it look like? An organization with a true kaizen mindset is one that is always striving to improve what it does; at every level. Everyone shares a common belief that a major part of their role in the business is to improve no only what they do as individuals, but also what the organization does as a whole. The conversations about improvement are not separate discussions held in a meeting room; they are a constant part of the dialogue. These organizations have a clear understanding of their purpose, who their customers are and what they want. They constantly look for small ideas and innovative ways to increase the value to the customer.

There are eight key requirements that are necessary to create a kaizen culture or mindset in any organization. The order of implementation is not critical, however from my experience you will achieve faster success by implementing in the order they are written. You won't necessarily have better success, but it will likely be faster and more efficient. The seven keys are:

1) Top level drive and belief
2) Management level buy-in

3) In-house dedicated resources
4) Management accountability
5) Recognition of performance and achievements
6) Program Development, What Program?
7) Knowledge Sharing

1. Top Level Drive and Belief

This may seem pretty obvious, however this is the biggest reason organizations begin the lean journey and fail to realise the benefits. There are two elements to this step and requirement. The first is drive from the top level and should be quite easy to achieve; the second is top level belief in the lean framework and tools, this is often more difficult to achieve. For the purpose of this text, I'll be referring to the top level as the CEO; in reality, the top level is the top hierarchy of the business.

Let's start with top level drive. What does it mean and how is it achieved?

We'll break this down into three topics:

1) Top level drive

2) Top level support

3) Top level belief

Top level drive

Top level drive is the best case scenario for any organization. Often the CEO will read or hear about lean and see it as an opportunity to 'get on the bandwagon' by implementing a lean program or activity. The CEO may get in an 'expert' to give a talk or hold a workshop with some of the management. There will be a flurry of activity with suggestion boxes being rolled out. Lean programs will kick off in an ad hoc manner, some of these may be successful and identify or even realise some improvements. There will be some new buzzwords and posters put up to advertise the new concepts; Japanese words will be a part of the latest lingo. People will start talking about culture, continuous improvement, Toyota etc. There may be new teams developed with names like kaizen team, CI group and facilitators running workshops. Usually, after a few months of activity, the buzz slowly reduces until the program quietly disappears. Often, the cycle will start again in a few years time and the process will repeat.

If this is the situation in your organization, then I wish you luck; lots of luck, because you'll need it. This is not what is meant by top level drive. This is more of a top level direction or order and in these circumstances it becomes the responsibility of those further down the hierarchy to deliver the program (often much further down).

Top level drive is where the responsibility of the outcomes sits with the CEO. Having the responsibility at the top of the hierarchy has a number of benefits, including:

1. This person is actively involved in the improvement program. They "lead from the front" and act as a role model for others in the organization (across all levels).

2. The old motto "the buck stops here" is true for this person. At the very least they will report to a board, or they may be the final level of reporting. Whichever way your organization is structured, any outcomes – positive or negative will reflect on the performance of this person.

3. If they are true leaders and are leading from the front, then you have the beginnings of a culture shift.

This all leads us to a situation where the CEO or top level executive is pulling the organization along the improvement journey; rather than pushing. With the CEO pulling rather than pushing, the next level of the organization is more likely to follow and themselves become drivers of the program as this is "the way we do things here". This continues down the hierarchy; obviously not everyone will buy in to the program and ideas but you will realize far more buy in through top level drive than without it – far more!

Top level support

So how does support differ from drive? Where drive is all about strong leadership, support is about empowerment. Support from the top level is evident when the people responsible for improvements (whether dedicated resource or managers/coordinators) also have the authority to both make decisions and to hold others accountable.

Every manager has a certain amount of authority, however what we mean here is the delegated authority of the CEO. Without this authority it will be difficult to make significant long term change. This is particularly true when discussing a dedicated lean or CI resource. They need the delegated authority of the CEO or equivalent. Short term gains can be made without this authority and sometimes you may even achieve the odd long term success; these are exceptions however and not the rule. We'll discuss the support required by the dedicated resource in a later chapter; here we will focus on the support required by the rest of the organization.

There are a number of ways the authority can be delegated; these include:

- Generic communication to entire organization
- Specific, targeted communication to project groups
- Continuous communication of delegation

By far the most effective method of communication is the continuous communication of delegation. By continuous, it doesn't mean to constantly remind people in the organization that you have the delegated authority; what is meant is that the CEO in their discussions reiterate when necessary that the project leaders are working with their authority.

With this support in place the projects can be run without the political playmaking threatening to take over. This will result in more efficient project delivery and more effective outcomes. You may have already experienced an improvement project without this support and know first-hand how frustrating the political game can be and how it can destroy the project.

Top Level Belief

So far we have discussed both top level drive and support. Now we are discussing top level belief; what it is and how it can assist in the delivery of your projects.

Top level belief is achieved when the top level of the organization has a high level of understanding of lean methodology. This understanding will empower the CEO to become fully engaged in the improvement program. The high level of understanding will become a belief once they have experienced for themselves how effective lean can be. This belief will elevate both top level drive and support to a higher degree than the methods discussed earlier.

Obviously not every CEO who is exposed to lean will become a believer. This will depend on the individual and the experiences they have been through; however the discussions held within the organization will also play a big part in this. If you (as a lean specialist) can promote the positives of lean across the organization, the discussions will be more positive and will influence people's beliefs.

As a lean specialist it is your role to not only embed the lean philosophies and tools into the organization, it is also critical that you play your part in developing a positive culture around the management system. This can be achieved through informal conversations, formal activities and marketing materials. An effective method is to organize site visits to similar organizations with mature and effective lean methods embedded. This is a good method that can be used for all levels of the organization. For the top level it can be effective to have them attend industry forums where other executives are speaking on the topic.

2. Management Level Buy-in

So what is different about the senior level management and why do they require different strategies to the top level? Firstly, they play a very different part in fostering a kaizen mindset from the top level. Whereas the top level are drivers and supporters of kaizen, this group is more actively involved in the program as they are working on the business and leading their teams.

Leadership may be an over used term in business books, however with the risk of digressing too far off topic I'll briefly discuss the importance of leadership on your improvement initiatives – this discussion will be in the form of two examples, see if you can pick which example had good lean leadership from the management level. I've used examples with similar deliverable for both examples to keep it consistent.

Example 1)

Visual Management Introduction

This example (let's call it introduction) had the scope of implementing a visual management system into an existing factory with very little current visual management in place.

External consultants were brought into the facility to run the project. The consultants met with management to understand their objectives and deliverables. The main objectives were to highlight when things were not going to plan – this could be either quantity or quality.

From there the consultants spent time with the teams on the shop floor asking questions about the processes before leaving the shop floor and returning to their offices to design the visual management boards.

Once designed, a mock up was completed and presented to the management team for approval which was granted after modifications and clarification. The boards were then finished for each area and wheeled onto the shop floor overnight, between shifts. The next day when the shift commenced the operators noticed the new boards that were in the way of the machinery and removed the boards from the factory in compliance with the corporate OHS policy.

A number of hours later, a senior executive visited the shop floor to inspect the new visual management system that he had been told (by a lower level manager) was operational. To his surprise he couldn't see any visual management in place. The executive then asked an operator where he could find the new visual management system; after some discussion, the operator realized he was talking about the boards that he and others had moved outside earlier so continued to lead the executive through the factory, outside where the new boards were sitting in the elements.

I'm sure you can imagine the senior executive was not impressed with the outcome.

Example 2)

Visual Management Introduction

This example (let's call it integration) also had a scope to introduce visual management into a factory where previously there had been very little and even less effective.

On this occasion the team leader approached the manager with some ideas to improve performance. One of the ideas was visual management; they were not experts, however had seen it in operation during some site visits. The manager and team leader approached the continuous improvement leader and a project plan was developed which was presented to the executive leadership group as a business case with estimated costings and timings for implementation. The business case was approved and funding approved pending final costings.

Initial kick off meeting was held with all staff working in the area and all staff impacted by the project. This meeting was held to discuss why the project was going ahead and what the project would look and feel like; what their involvement would be and what the responsibilities of the team leader, manager and CI Leader were. Members of the executive leadership were present and spoke at this kick off.

After this meeting a number of workshops were facilitated by the CI Leader with the Manager, Team Leader and groups of operators were held to ensure a sound understanding of requirements was there and also to gain consensus on the solutions. These workshops were a combination of 'classroom' and shop floor, hands on exercises.

Processes and work tasks were reviewed and modified where required to incorporate the visual management system to ensure the new system did not become a burden to the operators. Mock up boards were put up in the areas and the OHS team were requested by the manager to assist in undertaking a risk analysis to ensure no new risks were introduced.

Once all of the above was completed, the boards and systems were introduced, a lunch was put on for the factory both as a reward for their work in developing the system and to close off the project and introduce the new system (the CEO and Operations Manager both served the food at the lunch).

Performance in the area increased considerably and the demand for the system to be rolled out across the factory were so high, operators from the original area assisted in the delivery of further systems.

I'm sure you will agree that the second example provided a better outcome in many ways:

- Leadership
- Support / drive from executive level
- Manager buy-in

- Team engagement
- Improved performance

These examples are both real occurrences that I have witnessed in recent years and show that the way an organization views improvement can have a dramatic impact on the results. The examples also show how the behaviors of different levels of the organization can effect a culture change through their actions.

Back to the original comment; leadership is not up to any single person to facilitate, but is everyone's responsibility to play their part. Management is a different issue.

So, back to Management Level Buy-in. In the two examples provided, there were two very different management styles employed and the outcomes were just as different. The poor outcomes of example one cannot be blamed solely on the manager, however a major portion of the problem lies at their feet. It is really basic and it pains me to point it out, however the fact that I see these poor actions too often to ignore. A managers role is to enable their staff to perform at their highest capacity and capability; if you can achieve this as a manager your team will make you look good.

If you are a manager, you need to believe in what you are selling to your team; if you don't believe in it, do more research to either 1) believe in it, or 2) prove to the hierarchy they are not doing the right thing. It's your job as a manager to do this for your team.

If you are a higher level manager or executive and your managers are not buying in the same applies, and if you believe and it is the right thing to do, then you have to find a better way of selling it! Remember WIIFM – what's in it for me! Show them the benefits.

3. Dedicated Resources

Many organizations have dedicated resources for the implementation of their lean or continuous improvement program. You will notice throughout this book that the dedicated resources are referred to by a number of different titles; the term 'dedicated resource' can only be written so many times so I have used some of the many titles that the role can carry. The team size and structures varies greatly depending on the size, structure and needs of the organization. Some organizations outsource the facilitation and / or project management, while others outsource the entire operation. So what is the best structure?

That is a difficult question to answer as there is no 'one size fits all'. There are different models that can be applied and molded to any organization. There are also models that are proven not to work and others that can work with reliance on the people involved. The following pages will discuss the pro's and con's of a number of different models.

Dedicated Team

This model has a team usually consisting of a manager and officers/engineers. The responsibilities of the team can range from:

- Training and facilitation only

- Training, facilitation and project management

- Playing a de facto manager role during the course of the project

- Shared role of facilitation and project management with the department manager

Of the above structures, the last (shared role) is the most effective from my experiences. You will see I am a strong believer in management involvement, this will be explained further at the end of this chapter. By employing the shared role method, the facilitator can mentor the manager, train the staff, play a leading hand in driving the project with the manager present and accountable for the outcomes. While this may be more workload for the facilitator, the long term benefits are worth it.

The third scenario (de facto manager) can work well in some circumstances, particularly where the manager of a department is away for a period of time. This can provide an opportunity for a lean practitioner to come into the team and make some real changes along with some cultural change before handing back a higher performing team to the incumbent manager. It's important to have open and clear discussions with the manager before their absence to setup a clear understanding of what the lean practitioner will be doing and what this will mean to the manager on return; particular time must be spent with the manager setting expectations prior to leaving the department. Alternatively, the existing manager can be moved the area permanently in the case of low capabilities to learn or manage (if this is the situation, you have bigger problems than just implementing lean and should look at your management structure and skills)

The first two scenarios can work in an environment where the manager has a strong understanding of the lean principles and tools, meaning the facilitator can be utilized as a trainer and the manager can drive the change.

With a dedicated team deployed in an organization, it must be decided what size and how to use the team members. If the size of the organization permits, it is best to align the lean team members to divisions or departments in the organization. This enables the lean team members to work closely within a smaller part of the business to gain a closer and deeper understanding of its processes, structure, purpose etc. This will enable greater value to be gained from the lean facilitator.

Many organizations start with a single practitioner to "test the waters" before going further to develop a team (or possibly cease the journey). I can understand the reasons for this approach, however often it doesn't provide the benefits expected for a number of reasons:

- Lack of resources and high demand for skills means the facilitator is unable to give sufficient focus to any single activity to be successful.

- Due to the above issues, a bad culture towards lean develops. This can be both at the shop floor and management level.

- The single resource is likely to leave the role or the organization before significant improvements have been achieved.

If "testing the waters" is the approach your organization feels is necessary, I would recommend contracting a specialist group for a time period with agreed scope of works and measures to prove the potential (more on this shortly).

In-house or external resources?

This question was used in the opening paragraph of this chapter and as I said then it is difficult to answer which is best – this really depends on the situation. There is no doubt in my mind that internal resources are the best option in the perfect circumstances. These perfect circumstances are not available or present in all organizations. I will discuss the pro's and con's for both and you can determine which is best for your organization and current situation.

External Contractors:

There are many consulting firms offering Lean Consulting services, these services range from training right through to facilitating change programs. The pro's and con's below are based on the assumption of some facilitation work.

Pro's:

- You can access expertise that would otherwise be out of reach to a smaller organization or a business starting out on the lean journey.

- No requirement for new internal or permanent staff. This can make "selling" the idea easier to the board or parent company. It can even eliminate the need for the approval (which is not a good thing. Going lean should never be a secret or "hush hush" journey).

- Existing staff can continue working on the normal day to day operations of the business (once again, lean should become a part of the normal day to day business)

- This method can be used to coach / mentor managers to enable them to drive future lean endeavors.

Cons:

- This approach lacks management buy-in. Paying for an external resource can be seen as a short term fix and lack of true commitment.

- The contractors will take time to know your business. They cannot be expected to walk in and deliver results without know your business, customers, goals and risks etc.

- Contractors do not have any buy-in to your organization. Sure they are being paid to deliver, and they should deliver, however they do not have a vested interest in the success of your organization.

- They can easily walk away at the end of the contract, without the responsibility of seeing through the longer term improvements.

Internal Resources:

The use of dedicated internal resources can provide better long term benefits with the correct structure in place. The pro's and con's below are based on the assumption an internal dedicated resource is working in conjunction with the business managers.

Pro's:

- Indicates commitment from business to long term successes.

- The resource has a vested interest in the success of the business.

- The right resource will have a better understanding of the business and the impacts of change on other areas.

- The resource is accessible after the handover of projects.

Con's:

- Having dedicated internal resources can have the effect of reducing the responsibility of the managers.

- It can be difficult to identify the resources and skill set internally, resulting in the need to employ from external market. This will reduce the specific business knowledge of the resource in the short term.

- Dedicated resource can become overburdened. A program should be developed to manage the rollout.

From the pro's and con's it look quite balanced, however the negatives from contracting the service outweigh the positives. It is important that lean is looked at as a business model and not a short term opportunity or cost cutting exercise. The use of contractors adds to this short term view. I would recommend the development of internal dedicated resources; if your organization cannot afford this, then try harder to find the funding; if funding is still an issue resort to external contractors / consultants with a view to developing the internal resources.

In my opinion, regardless of the model employed, the critical factor for success is to make the managers responsible for the outcomes; not the lean facilitators or even the lean manager. The ownership needs to sit with the department managers. Obviously you need to have accountability through the dedicated resources, but this should be for the facilitation and opportunities, not the entirety of the outcomes. The management needs to be involved in the process to increase buy-in, eliminate push back after completion, create improvement culture and develop skills across the organization. This is discussed further in the next chapter.

4. Management Accountability

A mistake I see many organizations make is to employ a dedicated resource or team of resources to rollout a lean or continuous improvement program across the business without setting clear responsibilities and accountability for the outcomes. Just as many organizations are incorporating OHS responsibilities in all employees position descriptions (the smarter organizations are not using generic statements), we should be including business improvement responsibilities for all employees, especially managers.

At different levels of the business there needs to be clear business improvement responsibilities, the most important level to get right is the manager level.

Managers should be working on the business!

Many of the managers I have worked with spend far too much time working in the business rather then on it. This leaves them with far too little time available for short term strategic planning. What is the purpose of a manager? Whilst his is different in every organization, I see a manager's major priority being to enable their team to perform to their full potential. This means a manager needs to:

- Ensure sufficient resources to perform the work

- Ensure the availability of skills and technical knowledge

- Development of staff and team skills through mentoring, coaching and formal processes

- Eliminating the noise from the team's periphery to enable concentration to tasks

- Continuous improvement analysis and delivery of the activities and processes

- Monitor team and individual performance

- Lead the team in problem identification and root cause analysis

- Short, medium and long term strategic planning

The above over and above any technical and operational activities. Depending on what level of management we are talking about, the manager should spend between 50% and 80% of their time as an enabler and working on the business.

Too many managers I have seen have been promoted beyond their current capabilities and never take the time or make the effort to increase their capabilities. They may be technical experts or hard workers; however this doesn't make someone a good manager. This problem is largely created and compounded by the senior management that originally promoted them beyond their capability so the Manager in question cannot be held solely responsible for the resulting situation.

Responsibilities for improvements

It is important for both the Managers and the Lean / CI resource to have clearly defined roles and responsibilities in both driving the change and in the results from the program. If these roles and boundaries are not clearly defined, it will be difficult to achieve long term success as confusion will result.

So who should be responsible for what? It is important in any business area to achieve a cohesive team relationship. There are many books on breaking down silos in organizations on the market so it appears to be a wide spread problem. One of the biggest factors in creating these silo's is the lack of clear roles and responsibilities; if people don't know where the boundaries in their role are one of two things will occur:

1) One or both parties will overstep the perceived boundaries. This will result in a strained working relationship between the parties which will further lead to them not collaborating and in fact working separately.

2) Due to the confusion of no clear responsibilities being set there is a potential for neither party to get the work done or make the important decisions as each is waiting for the other.

The first rule in setting up the roles and responsibilities is to determine your approach before you set out and employ your lean resource. The second rule is to standardise your approach and be consistent in its delivery across the organization. If the approach is different across the organization you will create confusion and potentially distrust in the program. If a change of approach is required, the reasons and changes must be openly communicated. The third rule is to be open and clear with the communication; my rule is always to tell the team everything I can, not just what I think they should know!

Back to the question of who should be responsible for what; well let's look at each responsibility.

The Program Delivery

It will be no surprise that the CI Manager is the person responsible for the successful delivery of the overall improvement program. Obviously the management team, across all levels plays a major and important role in the success by providing support, drive and authority. The CI Manager is also responsible for the program planning and reporting for the improvement program.

The Individual Project Success

The success of each individual project should be the responsibility of the area manager, not the CI Manager. If the responsibility sits with the CI resources there is no accountability on the manager to improve the teams performance. If there is no requirement to improve something then there wouldn't be a project to be responsible for. This responsibility is no more than the usual business improvement requirements of any manager position and should be written into position descriptions.

The Team Performance

The improvement of the team has to be a major component of the manager's efforts and should be measured. Even outside of an improvement project this should be one of each manager's responsibilities; depending on the level of the manager in the corporate structure, they should spend up to 80% of their time working on the business rather than working in the business. Yes some technical knowledge can help, however if the team has a high level of knowledge and the manager is effective in enabling the team to perform to their combined capabilities then you will have a good chance at success.

Coaching and Mentoring

Both the area manager and the CI resources play their part in coaching and mentoring the team during the project and beyond.

The CI resources need to coach and mentor both the manager and the team in the lean tools, philosophies and habits. The area manager is responsible for coaching their team to approach the improvement journey with the right positive attitude during the project; they then need to ensure the team continues practicing the lean thinking after the completion of the project to make lean a part of their every day work.

Give your managers the tools to succeed and hold them accountable for the successes and failures of their teams and they might surprise you. You may find they are more capable than they have been credited with in the past and take your business to the next level. Every businesses most important asset is its people, are you respecting yours? Every level of the business is important to its success, however in my opinion, the manager level plays the critical enabling role and therefore needs to be empowered and capable.

5. Recognition of success

Every management book or course notes the importance of recognizing and celebrating the teams successes but many businesses and managers still don't do this very well.

This is what I see at many businesses:

- A BBQ lunch
- Catered lunch
- Lunch at the local bar or restaurant
- Certificate and gift voucher
- Presentation

The above list just isn't good enough and should be a part of the normal team building and promotion without having to achieve any extra successes. I am not a fan of the usual celebrations because they always feel fake or insincere from my experiences. Yes, have these team building exercises regularly but don't call them celebrations unless there is something big to celebrate and then make it special!

So what is the best way to recognize team success? Firstly, you will notice I didn't write individual success, this is because in most businesses the team is more important than the individuals and it has to be for the business to succeed. Individual recognition can be saved for the one on ones and performance reviews and is important, don't think I'm saying it's not; but not as important in most circumstances as the team success and recognition.

I have a different view to many practitioners and management consultants; I'm not a fan of the usual fanfare. My approach is more regular small recognition to the team; rather than occasional large scale celebration of the team. You'll notice I said "recognition to team", with emphasis on the word "to". While I do promote the success of my teams to the rest of the organization, the celebration and recognition is kept for the team themselves. Many people may not agree with my approach, and that is perfectly ok, this works for me and has worked for the teams I have worked with to maintain the hunger for success and build morale.

I am a big advocate for visual management; used effectively visual management provides so many positives. This book isn't about visual management but I believe it does play a big part in creating the kaizen mindset that it needs some discussion. Visual management can be used in many different ways including:

- Department / area signage to clearly define and identify work areas
- A visual aid for housekeeping and 5S
- Problem identification
- Displaying workload
- Visualization of targets and takt time
- Storyboards for promotion of activities

It is possible to overdo visual management (many would disagree) by either overuse or by misuse. Overuse is what we call 'wallpaper' and is where the walls of the organization become covered by 'visual management' to the point that it becomes clutter. Well before it gets to this point, the benefits have been lost to the entire organization; management and hands on staff. Misuse can be quite varied and includes:

- Undefined or unclear purpose of communication

- Inaccurate information or data

- Out of date information or data

- Lack of defined responsibilities

Either way, whether it is misused or overused, unless it is well managed (like everything) visual management will not be effective. Conversely a well managed visual management system can help you realize many benefits:

- High impact on organizational culture

- Improved morale

- Improved individual, team and organizational performance

- Early identification of problems

- Increased skill levels

- Waste identification and reduction / elimination

A much more detailed explanation of different visual management types and techniques will be in book seven of this series "Your 60 Minute Lean Business – The Tools" due for release in 2014; for now, let's look at how I use visual management to recognize the success of my teams.

Earlier in this chapter I mentioned that I recognize and celebrate the successes quite differently to many other managers and practitioners. What I will be explaining in the following pages is likely to be familiar to many readers, however may not be thought of in the same way.

Step 1 – Set Targets

The first thing that must be done is to set targets. No matter what type of business you are in, targets can be set for most activities. By setting targets you are also creating a structure of accountability; something that is often missing or lacking structure in many businesses.

Before you go and set targets for every activity, it is important to determine what the key activities are in the area you want to improve; this could be at an organizational level, at a work cell level or any level in between. Don't waste too much time on this; if you initially choose the wrong activities you can always change them at any time.

When setting targets there are a number of factors to consider; not all of these are relevant to every business or every situation:

- Production or throughput requirements

- Takt time

- Cycle time

- Resource allocation / availability

- Quality requirements

- External and internal influences such as other departments and / or external bodies

Targets should be SMART in that they are specific, measurable, achievable, relevant and time based. This sounds like commonsense but let's break this down a little further to understand why.

Specific – It must be very clear exactly what is being measured.

Measurable – Sounds obvious right? There must be an efficient method for measurement to ensure the data integrity waste isn't built into the reporting systems.

Achievable – A target set too high that is not achievable will have an adverse effect, yet a target too easily reached will not affect improvement.

Relevant – what you are measuring should relate to a problem or lead to a decision.

Time based – the higher the frequency the more often you can make adjustments. The frequency needs to be often enough to enable the right decisions at the right time.

Example:

Recently I was working with a team in a service industry; there was no production as such, however there was throughput of documentation. Forms and applications of many different types were received by the team and processed. There were different requirements for the times to process the different forms – these requirements were either regulatory or self imposed. When I first started working with the team many of the form types were behind in processing.

The first thing we did was to quantify and prioritize the work ahead of us. This was the easy part however, as many of you may have found in your own businesses, it can be a challenge drawing all of this information from people due to the fear of both repercussions and the unknown road ahead. Luckily this team was very open and forthcoming with the data. I made sure of recognizing this honesty publicly and to senior management; it is important this type of honesty is recognized and not used as ammunition for penalizing previous poor performance, unless the performance was negligence.

After we had prioritized the activities we needed to set daily targets to track our performance and recovery. There were no standardized work practices in place, not even any cycle times. So we went about measuring the cycle times; using these cycle times and the allocated resource time for the activities to set daily targets for both the recovery period and normal daily throughput to ensure a relapse of the situation did not occur.

Step 2 – Communication

After the targets have been set it is time to communicate them. Obviously, it is critical to communicate the targets to the staff responsible for achieving them, however it is just as important to communicate the targets with a wider audience.

Firstly, peripheral team members (those within the team but not responsible for meeting the target) need to understand what the targets are and what they mean to both those responsible and the greater team.

Secondly, members of supporting and / or customer / supplier teams within the business need to understand the targets and the impacts they have on the teams ability to be successful. This will also have a positive influence on the culture by improving cross departmental working relationships and break down the silos.

The communication needs to be clear, engaging and most importantly, it must be meaningful. The communication should leave all involved with a clear understanding of what is required and their role in achieving it. You have to find the best method to do this; different teams and situations require different approaches, it is up to you as a manager to identify the best communication methods and styles.

Some ideas for communication include:

- Town hall meetings
- Team meetings
- Toolbox meetings
- Email / digital billboards
- Visual management

A combination of different methods is usually best; if we look back at the example from step one we can look at how different methods have been used.

Example:

We identified a number of different groups that we needed to communicate the targets to.

Responsible team:

The team responsible for achieving the targets was involved in the setting of them, meaning they were all very aware of what was required and what it meant to them. Discussions were held to define who, within the team, would be responsible for data recording and analysis, the team leader was made responsible for daily toolbox meetings to discuss adherence to the targets.

The team responsibilities were documented and shared with the entire team.

Peripheral team members:

The other members of the team were brought into the discussion and were made aware of the targets. Although they had little or no direct impact on the activity, their support was needed by being aware of the impact the activities they perform could have on the target team.

This was communicated through a team meeting and further reinforced with email and visual communication.

Support Teams and departments:

Team members from other supporting departments and supplier departments were made aware of the target and the support required from them was outlined. This was communicated between the managers and coordinators of the respective teams and filtered to the team members.

Senior Management:

As the activity in question was a critical business process and had been under the close scrutiny of senior management the communication was extended to include this section of the organization. Email communication was sent to the senior management team when the targets were defined and throughout the measurement and reporting of the recovery.

Step 3 – Display

So you have set you targets and have communicated the expectations to the teams and the organization as required. Many people will now just get on with the job of achieving the targets; from my experiences this step is one of the most important in being successful.

In many businesses I have worked with, the managers are surprised at the amount of improvement this single step can realise. Often with no change to the existing targets or the processes an improvement of 30% or more is realised. How can just displaying the targets make that much difference; it's psychological! I believe humans have an instinct to succeed, this is why we are the dominant species on the planet. If we know what success means, most of us will do whatever we can to achieve it; it's that simple.

I mentioned earlier about the overuse of visual management; whatever you do to display the targets it must have an impact. I like to have visual management areas within the work cell where most of the targets and measures are displayed. In the situation of a new critical or significantly modified and important target I would locate it away from the standard visual management board to increase the impact ad awareness.

I like to keep the display type consistent to make it easier to read and get an understanding of the situation without spending too much time deciphering the data. For this reason I simply use old fashioned bar charts, however any type of chart can be used; the main point here is to use charts rather than words wherever possible; even in the explanations. In today's technological world it is now much cheaper to use electronic scoreboards to display and measure against your targets. A simple counter displaying the actual next to the target is very effective.

While an electronic counter is a good way to visualize the live actual against the target I still like a bar chart to show the trend over time. The team leader should be the person responsible for completing the trend chart; this will make sure they know what is happening and where the current performance is.

Step 4 – Measure

This should be the easy step, however there are a few things to keep in mind. Firstly, the measurement against your targets needs to be very low effort and should have minimal effect on the efficiency of the process you are measuring.

When measuring throughput, it is quite simply a measurement of the items produced or actioned (in a service industry). A simple method for monitoring throughput without adding effort is for the output to be placed in receptacles that hold a set number of pieces. This eliminates the need for the operator to count production. Another option is to build in an automatic counter into the production system; this can be quite a cost effective alternative in many process types. The best solution really depends on your business needs, the importance of the data accuracy and the volume in question.

But what if you are measuring something other than throughput, like quality? When measuring quality you will usually have an inspection step within the process. You can either record the frequency of pass / fail or you may decide to record the actual inspection result (dimension etc); this depends on the process and how critical the inspection point is.

If you choose to record the pass / fail frequency this is no different to the throughput methods. On the other hand, if you require the inspection results to be recorded you can either utilize a manual recording system such as a QA check sheet or an automatic recording system linked to the measurement equipment. The latter is capable of providing live run charts that can be used for analysis such as process capability etc.

These technology solutions for measuring and monitoring can provide high efficiency and consistency, however this comes at a cost. Whether you deploy a manual or automated system will depend on a number of factors:

- The accuracy required
- The availability of resources (capital and labour)

- The business type and volume of work

The number one rule is to make sure the system is fit for purpose.

Step 5 – Analysis and adjustments

Measurement should lead to analysis and decisions; either a decision to continue without change or a decision to make adjustments before or while continuing. If the data is not analyzed and is not required to be maintained for a contractual or regulatory requirement then you really should be asking why the measurement and data collection is undertaken and whether this should be continued.

Analysis of the data can take many forms; it may be as simple as hit / miss against throughput target or a pass / fail against quality target. Conversely, they may be far more detailed analysis looking at process capabilities, equipment and or resource efficiencies, financial performance and sustainability etc. The analysis methods used will depend on the critical nature of the process, the importance of the output and the business type and circumstances.

Through analysis of available data, educated and robust decisions and adjustments can be made. By including the team members in the analysis and the decision making you will not only be improving the skill set of the team through coaching, but also facilitating the deployment of the kaizen mindset.

Step 6 - Recognition

So how does all of this relate back to recognition? It's all in how you use the information and the opportunity. I see all visual data as an opportunity to develop the team; whether the data is positive or negative is almost irrelevant for this purpose. What is important is that the data is being used and there is frequent discussion with the team members.

If the data and outcome is positive you can obviously use this as a means to recognize the team's performance in successfully achieving the target. If the data and outcome is negative you can take the opportunity to develop the problem identification and root cause analysis skills of the team. By using the data, whether positive or negative in this way you are constantly recognizing the team.

In my opinion, the best recognition is when it comes for a senior member of the organization and it is at an unexpected time. By encouraging the senior management to walk the gemba, review the visual management boards and discussing the outcomes with the team members this important and effective recognition can become an ingrained part of your business.

This method of recognition will not only have a great impact on the team and organizational morale but also plays a key role in the development of your organization's kaizen mindset. Creating a culture of cross organization (both departmental and hierarchical) is a critical element of the kaizen mindset; a culture can only be developed through behaviors and discussions throughout the organization.

6. Program Development, What Program?

Lean is more than a program or series of projects; for a business to succeed with lean they need to make the tools, philosophies and practice an integrated part of the business practices. Lean is a management system and a way of doing business rather than a selection of tools and mismatched projects.

In the earlier book titled 7 Steps To A Lean Business I detailed the different methods of determining where to start your lean journey. Many businesses decide to introduce lean into the organization by fixing the squeaky wheel or the problem that is perceived to be the greatest at the time, before moving onto the next problem area. This concept may get you some quick wins on the board, however due to the haphazard approach it is unlikely the root causes of the problems will be properly identified and effectively resolved. Further to this point, it is most likely that in resolving one problem area you will become aware of the interactions and impacts of another area of the organization; these other areas could be customers, suppliers or stakeholders.

Lean Business Strategy

A lean business strategy is exactly what the name says. A strategy for developing a lean business will ensure the focus of the business activities is targeted towards efficient use of all resources; including:

- Staff

- Capital expenditure

- Operating expenditure

- Materials

- Consumables

All resource types are used to maximum efficiency and effectiveness. A lean business strategy will eliminate the fire fighting and keep the focus on identifying and eliminating waste.

While the term is a little daunting for many business leaders it really doesn't need to be. Every business has a strategy; most have many different strategies, this is just a matter of ensuring the strategies your organization has in place incorporate the philosophies and tools within this series of books. A lean business strategy isn't necessarily a standalone strategy; in fact it is probably best if it is not a standalone strategy and is in fact incorporated within all other organizational strategies. I have never found a business strategy that couldn't incorporate the lean philosophies and methodologies.

Back to the lean program development; the reason I started this chapter off by discussing the organizations strategies is that it is absolutely critical for a business to know where it is heading in order to develop a lean program. Any business development program requires a destination or road map; the strategies include this destination – a vision.

Once the organization has a vision, the program can be developed. It really is as simple as undertaking a gap analysis. Similar to the previous steps, this is an opportunity to continue to develop and embed the kaizen mindset throughout the organization.

Example

Say your organizations vision is to become the highest selling skateboard manufacturer in the country. The first thing you will notice is the goal is about sales, not production; now the two are very closely linked, however there are many businesses around the world with high wastage. Business is all about resources, high wastage results in reduced profits (resource). So you can be the highest producer without being the highest seller; and conversely you can be the highest seller without being the highest producer in any industry.

To eliminate the wastage (disposal of saleable stock) you can do a number of things, however the most efficient is effective market research. By knowing what the market (your potential customers) want you can make it; if you don't know what the market wants, you are guessing and will not always get it right – in fact you'll probably get it wrong more often than not..

A business that doesn't undertake effective market research will spend considerable time and money chasing the customer base while incurring wastage of saleable stock. This will result in reduced profit and often business failure. You will notice that in this example I have not looked at any step or activity between the market research and the sale of stock; yet even with this very limited detail we have seen how an approach of knowing the desired result before taking any action can be the difference between success and failure. This is the benefit of a strategy.

The above example is how a lean mindset can be applied to a startup business; now let's look at how a kaizen mindset can be applied to an established business.

Example 2

I'll continue with the skateboard manufacturer in this example, however this time the business is not a startup but is an existing business. Although the business is existing it is not achieving all of its goals. In this example, the business has the same vision of being the highest selling skateboard manufacturer in the country; however it is not achieving the goal.

After a number of years in business it is consistently finding itself ranked second to another manufacturer. The most frustrating part of the problem is they are manufacturing more than their competitors and the wholesale sales are higher; the problem is the returns are far, far too high. If they don't fix the problem in the near future, there will be irreparable damage to the brand; they don't have long to wait.

At least the first step towards fixing the problem has complete; defining the problem – poor product quality is costing sales, reducing profit and damaging the brand. Before they can jump in and fix the quality issues; they have to identify where in the production processes the issues are. They have to find the root cause.

By starting the search at the end of the process you can eliminate both causes of quality issues and eliminate waste within the processes as they are working towards identifying the root cause of the problem. Sometimes the root cause may be quite obvious; in these instances you can go straight to that part of the process and put in place the countermeasures.

The above examples show the importance of a vision – you can measure what you are achieving against the vision to identify gaps; once you have identified the gap you can put in place countermeasures. But lean isn't just about improving quality or increasing sales; it's really about eliminating waste. This is the reason why lean is not a program it is a journey towards the future state. For an organization to instill a kaizen mindset it must forget running stand alone projects and set itself a powerful vision. Set in place organizational strategies that empower the employees with strong leadership and a measurement system and culture that monitors the performance towards the vision.

So I'll finish this chapter off by answering the question in its name – there is no lean program. There is a lean journey! A lean or improvement program will not instill a kaizen mindset and can actually create a negative culture by losing sight of the value stream and encouraging silos.

7. Knowledge Sharing

Sharing the knowledge is a fundamental part of lean and is a key to developing a kaizen mindset. How do you go about sharing knowledge? Obviously you need to have knowledge before it can be shared; so the first step is to either a) buy in some knowledge or b) send existing staff out to get the knowledge. Both are legitimate options.

If you choose option b above there is no right or wrong way, however some ways are more effective than others. Going to a short course or similar isn't going to be very effective; neither is undertaking a certificate course really, you need experience. Most commercial centres have a chamber of commerce and many offer network groups to share knowledge between organizations. This option can be effective, however it will take more time than buying in the knowledge.

However you choose to get the knowledge, it is vital the knowledge is shared throughout the organization. This is best achieved by experiencing the knowledge rather than typical classroom training. The best advice I can give this is to refrain from reducing staff numbers through the journey; advice many organizations ignore unfortunately. There will come a time when the staff numbers can be reduced, however there are two reasons why you should wait to do this.

1) By not reducing staff numbers you will maintain morale (important to instill a kaizen mindset)

2) You will have resources to spread throughout the organization for the purpose of knowledge sharing.

The best method to share the lean knowledge is to expose as many staff as possible to experience the activities early in the journey. This involves including staff from other teams in the initial activities; this inclusion is critical to developing the right mindset. All activities should include:

- Team members from within the activity area

- Team leader of the activity area

- Team members from other business areas

- Team leaders from other business areas

- Management from across the organization

- Top level support

By including this cross organization mix of employees you will break down silos by building an awareness of each others work challenges and requirements. This approach will also get the discussions about lean going in the organization much faster than would otherwise be achievable.

During the initial activity, identify those participants who naturally understand the philosophies; these employees need to be nurtured into unofficial (or official) leaders. These become your lean army and can both communicate and influence others in the organization.

In the next activity make sure you follow the same approach with a good mix of employees; only this time include some of the 'army' you are developing. Not all of them, just a couple. This will further develop their skills while also building their confidence through experiencing what they are learning. Every activity you will identify some more natural talents; add these to the army and continue to include a selection in each and every activity.

This is a good way to share the skills and mindset internally, but there are also opportunities outside of the immediate business. If your business is part of a larger organization with a number of businesses, there could be opportunity for knowledge sharing across the different businesses. Then there is the opportunity to share the knowledge within your organization with other organizations that could be suppliers or customers. By influencing these external partners you will build better partnerships and working relationships while also creating opportunities to reduce some of the major wastes within the value stream.

8. Final Word

To close the topic off I'll share this story so you know when you the kaizen mindset is developing across the business.

A number of years ago, I was placed in charge of a low performing team in the organization I was working for. This team continuously missed their targets for both productivity and quality; this had been occurring for a number of years. I had a choice to either go in with guns blazing and make a change through fear or go in the department with the intention of sharing my knowledge and experiences. I chose the latter as I believe no employee goes to work to intentionally do a bad job; they just don't know how to do a better job.

I worked on the line with the team members and experienced all of the tasks over the first couple of weeks. This was done to gain their respect and to fully understand the challenges. It worked well; I identified a number of problems, both from within the team and from internal suppliers. I set about fixing one the major challenges being faced from an internal supplier; by bringing the team leader along for the discussions and workshops with the supplier manager and team leader.

This simple action empowered my team leader with the knowledge that I would back him up. We were on our way. Together, the team and I broke down all of the challenges, set up KPI's and a measurement system. Within three months they were one of the highest performing teams in the organization.

There were talks of poaching members of that team to spread across the business; I argued against this and instead we sent other team leaders and team members into that team to learn how they operated.